50 Breakfast Bowls to Start Your Day Right

By: Kelly Johnson

Table of Contents

- Acai Bowl with Granola
- Overnight Oats with Mixed Berries
- Mango Coconut Chia Pudding
- Peanut Butter Banana Smoothie Bowl
- Greek Yogurt and Fruit Bowl
- Sweet Potato Breakfast Bowl
- Chia Seed Pudding with Almond Butter
- Avocado Toast Bowl with Eggs
- Cinnamon Apple Oatmeal Bowl
- Tropical Smoothie Bowl
- Berry Quinoa Breakfast Bowl
- Banana Nut Oatmeal Bowl
- Chia Pudding with Kiwi and Coconut
- Almond Joy Overnight Oats
- Protein-Packed Smoothie Bowl
- Maple Pecan Granola Bowl
- Cinnamon Roll Oats Bowl
- Vegan Chocolate Peanut Butter Smoothie Bowl
- Mixed Berry Chia Pudding
- Banana Berry Oatmeal Bowl
- Green Smoothie Bowl with Spinach
- Cinnamon Apple Quinoa Bowl
- Pina Colada Smoothie Bowl
- Oats with Almonds and Raisins
- Blueberry Almond Butter Chia Bowl
- Yogurt Parfait Bowl with Granola
- Cherry Almond Breakfast Bowl
- Peach Coconut Oatmeal Bowl
- Chocolate Avocado Smoothie Bowl
- Strawberry Banana Overnight Oats
- Vegan Matcha Smoothie Bowl
- Raspberry Coconut Chia Pudding
- Apple Cinnamon Oats Bowl
- Tropical Acai Bowl with Pineapple
- Cocoa Coconut Oatmeal Bowl

- Baked Apple Oatmeal Bowl
- Kiwi Strawberry Chia Bowl
- Banana Chia Breakfast Pudding
- Peanut Butter and Jelly Overnight Oats
- Sweet Potato Quinoa Bowl
- Spicy Mango Chia Pudding
- Papaya Coconut Smoothie Bowl
- Almond Butter Banana Oats Bowl
- Spinach Avocado Smoothie Bowl
- Chocolate Chia Seed Pudding Bowl
- Pear Cinnamon Breakfast Bowl
- Tropical Fruit Yogurt Bowl
- Coconut Almond Oats Bowl
- Roasted Banana Oatmeal Bowl
- Acai and Almond Butter Smoothie Bowl

Acai Bowl with Granola

Ingredients:

- 1 packet frozen acai puree
- 1/2 banana, frozen
- 1/2 cup almond milk (or any milk of choice)
- 1 tbsp honey or agave (optional)
- Granola, sliced banana, and coconut flakes for topping

Instructions:

1. Blend the Acai Base: In a blender, combine frozen acai puree, frozen banana, almond milk, and honey/agave. Blend until smooth and thick.
2. Assemble the Bowl: Pour the acai mixture into a bowl.
3. Top the Bowl: Top with granola, sliced banana, and coconut flakes.
4. Serve: Enjoy immediately for a refreshing, nutrient-packed breakfast.

Overnight Oats with Mixed Berries

Ingredients:

- 1/2 cup rolled oats
- 1/2 cup almond milk (or any milk of choice)
- 1/2 cup Greek yogurt (optional for creaminess)
- 1 tbsp chia seeds
- 1/4 cup mixed berries (strawberries, blueberries, raspberries)
- 1 tsp honey or maple syrup (optional)

Instructions:

1. Prepare the Oats: In a jar or container, mix rolled oats, almond milk, Greek yogurt, chia seeds, and sweetener (if using).
2. Refrigerate Overnight: Seal the container and refrigerate for at least 4 hours or overnight.
3. Top with Berries: In the morning, stir the oats and top with mixed berries.
4. Serve: Enjoy chilled for a quick, nutritious breakfast.

Mango Coconut Chia Pudding

Ingredients:

- 1/2 cup coconut milk
- 2 tbsp chia seeds
- 1/2 cup fresh or frozen mango, diced
- 1 tbsp shredded coconut
- 1 tsp honey or agave (optional)

Instructions:

1. Prepare the Pudding: In a bowl, combine coconut milk, chia seeds, and honey/agave (if using). Stir well.
2. Refrigerate: Cover and refrigerate for at least 2 hours or overnight, allowing the chia seeds to absorb the liquid.
3. Assemble the Bowl: Once the pudding has thickened, top with diced mango and shredded coconut.
4. Serve: Enjoy chilled for a creamy and tropical breakfast.

Peanut Butter Banana Smoothie Bowl

Ingredients:

- 1 frozen banana
- 1 tbsp peanut butter
- 1/2 cup almond milk (or any milk of choice)
- 1/4 tsp cinnamon
- Granola and banana slices for topping

Instructions:

1. Blend the Smoothie Base: In a blender, combine frozen banana, peanut butter, almond milk, and cinnamon. Blend until smooth and thick.
2. Assemble the Bowl: Pour the smoothie into a bowl.
3. Top the Bowl: Add granola and banana slices on top.
4. Serve: Enjoy immediately for a creamy, protein-packed breakfast.

Greek Yogurt and Fruit Bowl

Ingredients:

- 1 cup Greek yogurt
- 1/4 cup mixed fresh fruit (berries, kiwi, banana)
- 1 tbsp honey or agave
- Granola for topping

Instructions:

1. Assemble the Bowl: Spoon the Greek yogurt into a bowl.
2. Add Fruit: Top with fresh mixed fruit.
3. Drizzle with Sweetener: Drizzle honey or agave on top.
4. Serve: Sprinkle with granola for crunch and serve immediately.

Sweet Potato Breakfast Bowl

Ingredients:

- 1 medium sweet potato
- 1/4 cup Greek yogurt (or dairy-free yogurt)
- 1 tbsp almond butter
- 1 tbsp chia seeds
- 1/4 tsp cinnamon
- 1 tbsp maple syrup (optional)

Instructions:

1. Prepare the Sweet Potato: Roast or microwave the sweet potato until tender. Peel and mash the flesh.
2. Assemble the Bowl: Spoon the mashed sweet potato into a bowl and top with Greek yogurt, almond butter, chia seeds, cinnamon, and a drizzle of maple syrup.
3. Serve: Enjoy warm or chilled for a filling, nutrient-dense breakfast.

Chia Seed Pudding with Almond Butter

Ingredients:

- 1 cup almond milk (or any milk of choice)
- 3 tbsp chia seeds
- 1 tbsp almond butter
- 1 tsp maple syrup or honey (optional)

Instructions:

1. Prepare the Pudding: In a bowl or jar, combine almond milk, chia seeds, almond butter, and maple syrup/honey (if using). Stir well.
2. Refrigerate: Cover and refrigerate for at least 2 hours or overnight.
3. Serve: Stir the pudding and top with additional almond butter or your favorite toppings like granola or fruit.

Avocado Toast Bowl with Eggs

Ingredients:

- 1 ripe avocado
- 1-2 eggs (fried, poached, or scrambled)
- 1 slice whole grain toast
- Salt and pepper to taste
- Red pepper flakes or hot sauce (optional)

Instructions:

1. Prepare the Avocado: Mash the avocado in a bowl and season with salt and pepper.
2. Prepare the Eggs: Cook the eggs to your preference (fried, poached, or scrambled).
3. Assemble the Bowl: Place the mashed avocado in a bowl and top with the cooked eggs. Add pieces of toasted whole grain bread.
4. Serve: Sprinkle with red pepper flakes or drizzle with hot sauce for an extra kick. Serve immediately.

Cinnamon Apple Oatmeal Bowl

Ingredients:

- 1/2 cup rolled oats
- 1 cup almond milk (or any milk of choice)
- 1 apple, diced
- 1/2 tsp cinnamon
- 1 tbsp honey or maple syrup
- Chopped nuts for topping (optional)

Instructions:

1. **Cook the Oats**: In a pot, bring almond milk to a simmer. Add oats and cook according to package instructions.
2. **Prepare the Apples**: While the oats are cooking, sauté the diced apple with cinnamon in a small pan until soft (about 5 minutes).
3. **Assemble the Bowl**: Once the oats are cooked, stir in the honey or maple syrup and top with the cinnamon apples.
4. **Serve**: Add chopped nuts on top for extra crunch. Serve immediately.

Tropical Smoothie Bowl

Ingredients:

- 1/2 cup frozen mango chunks
- 1/2 cup frozen pineapple chunks
- 1/2 banana
- 1/2 cup coconut milk (or any milk of choice)
- 1 tbsp chia seeds
- Sliced fruit for topping (banana, kiwi, mango)

Instructions:

1. **Blend the Smoothie**: In a blender, combine frozen mango, pineapple, banana, coconut milk, and chia seeds. Blend until smooth.
2. **Assemble the Bowl**: Pour the smoothie into a bowl.
3. **Top the Bowl**: Add sliced tropical fruits (banana, kiwi, mango) on top.
4. **Serve**: Serve immediately for a refreshing, nutrient-packed breakfast.

Berry Quinoa Breakfast Bowl

Ingredients:

- 1/2 cup cooked quinoa
- 1/2 cup mixed berries (strawberries, blueberries, raspberries)
- 1/4 cup almond milk (or any milk of choice)
- 1 tbsp honey or maple syrup
- Chopped almonds for topping

Instructions:

1. **Prepare the Quinoa**: Cook quinoa according to package instructions. Let it cool.
2. **Combine**: In a bowl, combine quinoa, almond milk, and honey. Stir well.
3. **Top the Bowl**: Add mixed berries and chopped almonds on top.
4. **Serve**: Serve immediately for a protein-rich, filling breakfast.

Banana Nut Oatmeal Bowl

Ingredients:

- 1/2 cup rolled oats
- 1 cup almond milk (or any milk of choice)
- 1 ripe banana, sliced
- 1/4 cup walnuts, chopped
- 1 tbsp honey or maple syrup
- 1/4 tsp cinnamon

Instructions:

1. **Cook the Oats**: In a pot, bring almond milk to a simmer. Add oats and cook according to package instructions.
2. **Assemble the Bowl**: Once the oats are cooked, stir in the sliced banana, cinnamon, and honey or maple syrup.
3. **Top the Bowl**: Add chopped walnuts on top.
4. **Serve**: Serve immediately for a warm, nourishing breakfast.

Chia Pudding with Kiwi and Coconut

Ingredients:

- 1/2 cup coconut milk (or any milk of choice)
- 2 tbsp chia seeds
- 1 tbsp honey or maple syrup
- 1/2 kiwi, sliced
- Shredded coconut for topping

Instructions:

1. **Make the Chia Pudding**: In a jar, combine coconut milk, chia seeds, and honey. Stir well, then refrigerate overnight or for at least 4 hours to thicken.
2. **Top the Pudding**: In the morning, top the chia pudding with sliced kiwi and shredded coconut.
3. **Serve**: Serve chilled for a refreshing, nutrient-packed breakfast.

Almond Joy Overnight Oats

Ingredients:

- 1/2 cup rolled oats
- 1/2 cup almond milk (or any milk of choice)
- 1 tbsp cocoa powder
- 1 tbsp shredded coconut
- 1 tbsp almond butter
- 1 tbsp maple syrup
- Chopped almonds for topping

Instructions:

1. **Prepare the Oats**: In a jar or container, combine oats, almond milk, cocoa powder, shredded coconut, almond butter, and maple syrup. Stir well.
2. **Refrigerate**: Cover and refrigerate overnight or for at least 4 hours.
3. **Top the Oats**: In the morning, top with chopped almonds for extra crunch.
4. **Serve**: Serve chilled for a chocolatey, nutty breakfast.

Protein-Packed Smoothie Bowl

Ingredients:

- 1/2 cup Greek yogurt
- 1/2 banana
- 1/2 cup frozen berries (strawberries, blueberries)
- 1 tbsp almond butter or peanut butter
- 1/4 cup protein powder (optional)
- Granola and sliced fruit for topping

Instructions:

1. **Blend the Smoothie**: In a blender, combine Greek yogurt, banana, frozen berries, almond butter, and protein powder. Blend until smooth.
2. **Assemble the Bowl**: Pour the smoothie into a bowl.
3. **Top the Bowl**: Add granola and sliced fruit on top.
4. **Serve**: Serve immediately for a filling, protein-packed breakfast.

Maple Pecan Granola Bowl

Ingredients:

- 1 cup Greek yogurt or almond milk (for a dairy-free option)
- 1/4 cup maple syrup
- 1/4 cup pecans, chopped
- 1/4 cup granola
- 1/2 banana, sliced

Instructions:

1. **Prepare the Base**: In a bowl, combine Greek yogurt or almond milk with maple syrup.
2. **Top the Bowl**: Add chopped pecans, granola, and sliced banana.
3. **Serve**: Serve immediately for a sweet, crunchy breakfast.

Cinnamon Roll Oats Bowl

Ingredients:

- 1/2 cup rolled oats
- 1 cup almond milk (or any milk of choice)
- 1/2 tsp cinnamon
- 1 tbsp maple syrup
- 1 tbsp chopped pecans or walnuts
- 1/4 tsp vanilla extract

Instructions:

1. **Cook the Oats**: In a pot, bring almond milk to a simmer. Add oats and cook according to package instructions.
2. **Flavor the Oats**: Stir in cinnamon, maple syrup, and vanilla extract once the oats are cooked.
3. **Top the Bowl**: Add chopped nuts on top for a cinnamon roll-inspired crunch.
4. **Serve**: Serve immediately for a warm, comforting breakfast.

Vegan Chocolate Peanut Butter Smoothie Bowl

Ingredients:

- 1/2 banana, frozen
- 1 tbsp peanut butter
- 1 tbsp cocoa powder
- 1/2 cup almond milk (or any milk of choice)
- 1/4 tsp vanilla extract
- 1 tbsp chia seeds
- Granola and sliced banana for topping

Instructions:

1. **Blend the Smoothie**: In a blender, combine frozen banana, peanut butter, cocoa powder, almond milk, vanilla extract, and chia seeds. Blend until smooth.
2. **Assemble the Bowl**: Pour the smoothie into a bowl.
3. **Top the Bowl**: Add granola and sliced banana on top for added texture.
4. **Serve**: Serve immediately for a creamy, chocolatey breakfast.

Mixed Berry Chia Pudding

Ingredients:

- 1/2 cup almond milk (or any milk of choice)
- 2 tbsp chia seeds
- 1 tbsp honey or maple syrup
- 1/2 cup mixed berries (strawberries, blueberries, raspberries)

Instructions:

1. **Make the Chia Pudding**: In a jar, combine almond milk, chia seeds, and honey. Stir well, then refrigerate overnight or for at least 4 hours.
2. **Top the Pudding**: In the morning, top the chia pudding with mixed berries.
3. **Serve**: Serve chilled for a nutritious, antioxidant-packed breakfast.

Banana Berry Oatmeal Bowl

Ingredients:

- 1/2 cup rolled oats
- 1 cup almond milk (or any milk of choice)
- 1/2 banana, sliced
- 1/2 cup mixed berries
- 1 tbsp chia seeds
- 1 tbsp honey or maple syrup

Instructions:

1. **Cook the Oats**: In a pot, bring almond milk to a simmer. Add oats and cook according to package instructions.
2. **Assemble the Bowl**: Once the oats are cooked, stir in honey or maple syrup.
3. **Top the Bowl**: Add sliced banana, mixed berries, and chia seeds on top.
4. **Serve**: Serve immediately for a delicious, fruity breakfast.

Green Smoothie Bowl with Spinach

Ingredients:

- 1/2 cup frozen mango chunks
- 1/2 banana
- 1 handful spinach
- 1/2 cup almond milk (or any milk of choice)
- 1 tbsp chia seeds
- Sliced fruit (banana, kiwi) for topping

Instructions:

1. **Blend the Smoothie**: In a blender, combine frozen mango, banana, spinach, almond milk, and chia seeds. Blend until smooth.
2. **Assemble the Bowl**: Pour the smoothie into a bowl.
3. **Top the Bowl**: Add sliced fruit on top for extra texture and flavor.
4. **Serve**: Serve immediately for a refreshing, nutrient-packed breakfast.

Cinnamon Apple Quinoa Bowl

Ingredients:

- 1/2 cup cooked quinoa
- 1/2 apple, diced
- 1/4 tsp cinnamon
- 1 tbsp maple syrup
- 1 tbsp chopped walnuts (optional)

Instructions:

1. **Prepare the Quinoa**: Cook quinoa according to package instructions. Let it cool.
2. **Prepare the Apples**: While the quinoa is cooking, sauté the diced apple with cinnamon in a small pan until soft (about 5 minutes).
3. **Assemble the Bowl**: Once the quinoa is cooked, add maple syrup and stir. Top with cinnamon apples and chopped walnuts.
4. **Serve**: Serve warm for a hearty, warming breakfast.

Pina Colada Smoothie Bowl

Ingredients:

- 1/2 cup frozen pineapple chunks
- 1/2 banana, frozen
- 1/2 cup coconut milk (or any milk of choice)
- 1 tbsp shredded coconut
- Granola for topping

Instructions:

1. **Blend the Smoothie**: In a blender, combine frozen pineapple, frozen banana, coconut milk, and shredded coconut. Blend until smooth.
2. **Assemble the Bowl**: Pour the smoothie into a bowl.
3. **Top the Bowl**: Add granola on top for extra crunch.
4. **Serve**: Serve immediately for a tropical, refreshing breakfast.

Oats with Almonds and Raisins

Ingredients:

- 1/2 cup rolled oats
- 1 cup almond milk (or any milk of choice)
- 1/4 cup raisins
- 1/4 cup chopped almonds
- 1 tbsp honey or maple syrup
- 1/4 tsp cinnamon

Instructions:

1. **Cook the Oats**: In a pot, bring almond milk to a simmer. Add oats and cook according to package instructions.
2. **Assemble the Bowl**: Once the oats are cooked, stir in cinnamon and honey or maple syrup.
3. **Top the Bowl**: Add raisins and chopped almonds on top for a sweet and crunchy texture.
4. **Serve**: Serve immediately for a hearty, comforting breakfast.

Blueberry Almond Butter Chia Bowl

Ingredients:

- 1/2 cup almond milk (or any milk of choice)
- 2 tbsp chia seeds
- 1 tbsp almond butter
- 1/2 cup blueberries
- 1 tbsp honey or maple syrup

Instructions:

1. **Make the Chia Pudding**: In a jar, combine almond milk, chia seeds, and almond butter. Stir well, then refrigerate overnight or for at least 4 hours.
2. **Top the Pudding**: In the morning, top with blueberries and drizzle with honey or maple syrup.
3. **Serve**: Serve chilled for a creamy, protein-packed breakfast.

Yogurt Parfait Bowl with Granola

Ingredients:

- 1 cup Greek yogurt (or dairy-free yogurt)
- 1/4 cup granola
- 1/2 cup mixed berries (strawberries, blueberries, raspberries)
- 1 tbsp honey or maple syrup (optional)
- A sprinkle of chia seeds or flaxseeds (optional)

Instructions:

1. **Assemble the Parfait**: In a bowl, layer Greek yogurt, granola, and mixed berries.
2. **Add Sweetener**: Drizzle with honey or maple syrup if desired.
3. **Top with Seeds**: Sprinkle chia seeds or flaxseeds on top for extra nutrition.
4. **Serve**: Serve immediately for a creamy, crunchy, and refreshing breakfast.

Cherry Almond Breakfast Bowl

Ingredients:

- 1/2 cup rolled oats
- 1 cup almond milk (or any milk of choice)
- 1/2 cup cherries, pitted and halved
- 2 tbsp sliced almonds
- 1 tbsp honey or maple syrup
- 1/4 tsp almond extract (optional)

Instructions:

1. **Cook the Oats**: In a pot, bring almond milk to a simmer. Add oats and cook according to package instructions.
2. **Assemble the Bowl**: Once the oats are cooked, stir in honey or maple syrup and almond extract.
3. **Top the Bowl**: Add cherries and sliced almonds on top.
4. **Serve**: Serve warm for a sweet, nutty, and fruity breakfast.

Peach Coconut Oatmeal Bowl

Ingredients:

- 1/2 cup rolled oats
- 1 cup coconut milk (or any milk of choice)
- 1/2 peach, sliced
- 1 tbsp shredded coconut
- 1 tbsp maple syrup or honey
- A sprinkle of cinnamon (optional)

Instructions:

1. **Cook the Oats**: In a pot, bring coconut milk to a simmer. Add oats and cook according to package instructions.
2. **Assemble the Bowl**: Once the oats are cooked, stir in maple syrup or honey and a sprinkle of cinnamon.
3. **Top the Bowl**: Add sliced peach and shredded coconut on top.
4. **Serve**: Serve immediately for a tropical, comforting breakfast.

Chocolate Avocado Smoothie Bowl

Ingredients:

- 1/2 avocado, peeled and pitted
- 1 banana, frozen
- 1 tbsp cocoa powder
- 1/2 cup almond milk (or any milk of choice)
- 1 tbsp almond butter (optional)
- Sliced bananas, granola, and cacao nibs for topping

Instructions:

1. **Blend the Smoothie**: In a blender, combine avocado, frozen banana, cocoa powder, almond milk, and almond butter. Blend until smooth.
2. **Assemble the Bowl**: Pour the smoothie into a bowl.
3. **Top the Bowl**: Add sliced bananas, granola, and cacao nibs on top.
4. **Serve**: Serve immediately for a creamy, chocolatey breakfast.

Strawberry Banana Overnight Oats

Ingredients:

- 1/2 cup rolled oats
- 1/2 cup almond milk (or any milk of choice)
- 1/4 cup strawberries, chopped
- 1/2 banana, sliced
- 1 tbsp chia seeds
- 1 tsp honey or maple syrup (optional)

Instructions:

1. **Make the Overnight Oats**: In a jar, combine rolled oats, almond milk, chia seeds, and honey or maple syrup. Stir well, cover, and refrigerate overnight.
2. **Add Fruit**: In the morning, top the oats with fresh strawberries and banana slices.
3. **Serve**: Serve chilled for a quick and delicious breakfast.

Vegan Matcha Smoothie Bowl

Ingredients:

- 1/2 banana, frozen
- 1/2 cup spinach
- 1 tsp matcha powder
- 1/2 cup almond milk (or any milk of choice)
- 1 tbsp almond butter
- Granola and chia seeds for topping

Instructions:

1. **Blend the Smoothie**: In a blender, combine frozen banana, spinach, matcha powder, almond milk, and almond butter. Blend until smooth.
2. **Assemble the Bowl**: Pour the smoothie into a bowl.
3. **Top the Bowl**: Add granola and chia seeds on top for added crunch and nutrition.
4. **Serve**: Serve immediately for a vibrant, energizing breakfast.

Raspberry Coconut Chia Pudding

Ingredients:

- 1/2 cup coconut milk (or any milk of choice)
- 2 tbsp chia seeds
- 1/2 cup raspberries
- 1 tbsp shredded coconut
- 1 tbsp honey or maple syrup (optional)

Instructions:

1. **Make the Chia Pudding**: In a jar, combine coconut milk, chia seeds, and honey or maple syrup. Stir well, then refrigerate overnight or for at least 4 hours.
2. **Top the Pudding**: In the morning, top the chia pudding with fresh raspberries and shredded coconut.
3. **Serve**: Serve chilled for a creamy, tropical breakfast.

Apple Cinnamon Oats Bowl

Ingredients:

- 1/2 cup rolled oats
- 1 cup almond milk (or any milk of choice)
- 1/2 apple, chopped
- 1/4 tsp cinnamon
- 1 tbsp maple syrup or honey
- Chopped walnuts or almonds for topping

Instructions:

1. **Cook the Oats**: In a pot, bring almond milk to a simmer. Add oats and cook according to package instructions.
2. **Add Flavor**: Stir in cinnamon and maple syrup or honey once the oats are cooked.
3. **Top the Bowl**: Add chopped apple and nuts on top.
4. **Serve**: Serve warm for a comforting and nutritious breakfast.

Tropical Acai Bowl with Pineapple

Ingredients:

- 1 acai packet (frozen)
- 1/2 cup pineapple chunks (fresh or frozen)
- 1/2 banana, frozen
- 1/2 cup coconut water or almond milk
- 1 tbsp chia seeds
- Granola, coconut flakes, and extra pineapple for topping

Instructions:

1. **Blend the Acai Base**: In a blender, combine acai packet, pineapple chunks, banana, and coconut water (or almond milk). Blend until smooth.
2. **Assemble the Bowl**: Pour the acai smoothie mixture into a bowl.
3. **Top the Bowl**: Add granola, coconut flakes, and extra pineapple on top for texture and extra tropical flavor.
4. **Serve**: Serve immediately for a refreshing and energizing breakfast.

Cocoa Coconut Oatmeal Bowl

Ingredients:

- 1/2 cup rolled oats
- 1 cup coconut milk (or any milk of choice)
- 1 tbsp cocoa powder
- 1 tbsp shredded coconut
- 1 tbsp honey or maple syrup
- Sliced banana or berries for topping

Instructions:

1. **Cook the Oats**: In a pot, bring coconut milk to a simmer. Add oats and cocoa powder, and cook according to package instructions.
2. **Add Sweetener**: Stir in honey or maple syrup for sweetness.
3. **Top the Bowl**: Add shredded coconut and sliced banana or berries on top.
4. **Serve**: Serve warm for a rich, chocolatey breakfast.

Baked Apple Oatmeal Bowl

Ingredients:

- 1/2 cup rolled oats
- 1 cup almond milk (or any milk of choice)
- 1 apple, peeled and chopped
- 1/2 tsp cinnamon
- 1 tbsp maple syrup or honey
- Chopped walnuts or almonds for topping

Instructions:

1. **Bake the Apples**: Preheat oven to 350°F (175°C). Place chopped apples on a baking sheet, sprinkle with cinnamon, and bake for 15 minutes.
2. **Cook the Oats**: In a pot, bring almond milk to a simmer. Add oats and cook according to package instructions.
3. **Assemble the Bowl**: Once oats are cooked, stir in maple syrup or honey and top with baked apples.
4. **Serve**: Add walnuts or almonds for crunch, and serve warm.

Kiwi Strawberry Chia Bowl

Ingredients:

- 1/2 cup coconut milk (or any milk of choice)
- 2 tbsp chia seeds
- 1/2 kiwi, peeled and sliced
- 1/4 cup strawberries, sliced
- 1 tbsp honey or maple syrup (optional)

Instructions:

1. **Make the Chia Pudding**: In a jar, combine coconut milk, chia seeds, and honey or maple syrup (if using). Stir well and refrigerate overnight or for at least 4 hours.
2. **Top the Pudding**: In the morning, top the chia pudding with sliced kiwi and strawberries.
3. **Serve**: Serve chilled for a fresh and fruity breakfast.

Banana Chia Breakfast Pudding

Ingredients:

- 1/2 cup almond milk (or any milk of choice)
- 2 tbsp chia seeds
- 1 ripe banana, mashed
- 1/2 tsp vanilla extract
- 1 tbsp maple syrup or honey

Instructions:

1. **Make the Chia Pudding**: In a jar, combine almond milk, chia seeds, mashed banana, vanilla extract, and maple syrup. Stir well, cover, and refrigerate overnight.
2. **Top the Pudding**: In the morning, give the pudding a good stir and top with sliced banana or nuts, if desired.
3. **Serve**: Serve chilled for a creamy, nutritious breakfast.

Peanut Butter and Jelly Overnight Oats

Ingredients:

- 1/2 cup rolled oats
- 1/2 cup almond milk (or any milk of choice)
- 1 tbsp peanut butter
- 1 tbsp fruit jam (such as strawberry or grape)
- 1/2 banana, sliced (optional)

Instructions:

1. **Prepare the Oats**: In a jar, combine rolled oats, almond milk, peanut butter, and fruit jam. Stir well and refrigerate overnight.
2. **Top the Oats**: In the morning, top the oats with sliced banana for added sweetness.
3. **Serve**: Serve chilled for a classic peanut butter and jelly flavor.

Sweet Potato Quinoa Bowl

Ingredients:

- 1/2 cup cooked quinoa
- 1/2 cup roasted sweet potato cubes
- 1/4 cup almond milk (or any milk of choice)
- 1/4 tsp cinnamon
- 1 tbsp maple syrup
- Chopped nuts (like pecans or walnuts) for topping

Instructions:

1. **Prepare the Sweet Potato**: Preheat the oven to 375°F (190°C). Roast sweet potato cubes with a drizzle of olive oil and cinnamon for 20 minutes, or until tender.
2. **Assemble the Bowl**: In a bowl, combine cooked quinoa and roasted sweet potato cubes. Stir in almond milk and maple syrup.
3. **Top the Bowl**: Add chopped nuts for extra crunch.
4. **Serve**: Serve warm for a hearty and filling breakfast.

Spicy Mango Chia Pudding

Ingredients:

- 1/2 cup coconut milk (or any milk of choice)
- 2 tbsp chia seeds
- 1/2 cup mango, chopped
- 1/4 tsp cayenne pepper
- 1 tbsp honey or maple syrup

Instructions:

1. **Make the Chia Pudding**: In a jar, combine coconut milk, chia seeds, honey or maple syrup, and cayenne pepper. Stir well, cover, and refrigerate overnight.
2. **Top the Pudding**: In the morning, top the chia pudding with fresh chopped mango.
3. **Serve**: Serve chilled for a spicy, sweet, and refreshing breakfast.

Papaya Coconut Smoothie Bowl

Ingredients:

- 1/2 papaya, peeled and chopped
- 1/2 cup coconut milk (or any milk of choice)
- 1/2 banana, frozen
- 1 tbsp shredded coconut
- 1 tbsp chia seeds
- Granola and extra papaya slices for topping

Instructions:

1. **Blend the Smoothie**: In a blender, combine papaya, coconut milk, banana, and shredded coconut. Blend until smooth and creamy.
2. **Assemble the Bowl**: Pour the smoothie mixture into a bowl.
3. **Top the Bowl**: Add chia seeds, granola, and extra papaya slices on top for texture and extra tropical flavor.
4. **Serve**: Serve immediately for a refreshing breakfast or snack.

Almond Butter Banana Oats Bowl

Ingredients:

- 1/2 cup rolled oats
- 1 cup almond milk (or any milk of choice)
- 1 tbsp almond butter
- 1/2 banana, sliced
- 1 tbsp chia seeds
- A drizzle of honey or maple syrup (optional)

Instructions:

1. **Cook the Oats**: In a pot, bring almond milk to a simmer. Add rolled oats and cook until soft and creamy.
2. **Add Almond Butter**: Stir in almond butter and a drizzle of honey or maple syrup for sweetness.
3. **Top the Bowl**: Add sliced banana and chia seeds on top.
4. **Serve**: Serve warm for a creamy and nourishing breakfast.

Spinach Avocado Smoothie Bowl

Ingredients:

- 1/2 avocado
- 1 handful spinach
- 1/2 banana, frozen
- 1/2 cup coconut water (or almond milk)
- 1 tbsp flax seeds or chia seeds
- Granola, nuts, or sliced fruits for topping

Instructions:

1. **Blend the Smoothie**: In a blender, combine avocado, spinach, frozen banana, coconut water, and flax seeds. Blend until smooth and creamy.
2. **Assemble the Bowl**: Pour the smoothie into a bowl.
3. **Top the Bowl**: Add granola, nuts, or fresh fruits like sliced bananas or berries on top.
4. **Serve**: Serve immediately for a nutritious and energizing breakfast.

Chocolate Chia Seed Pudding Bowl

Ingredients:

- 1 cup almond milk (or any milk of choice)
- 3 tbsp chia seeds
- 1 tbsp cocoa powder
- 1 tbsp maple syrup or honey
- Sliced strawberries, banana, or nuts for topping

Instructions:

1. **Make the Chia Pudding**: In a jar, combine almond milk, chia seeds, cocoa powder, and maple syrup. Stir well, cover, and refrigerate overnight.
2. **Top the Pudding**: In the morning, give the pudding a good stir and top with sliced strawberries, banana, or your favorite nuts.
3. **Serve**: Serve chilled for a rich and satisfying chocolatey breakfast.

Pear Cinnamon Breakfast Bowl

Ingredients:

- 1 pear, diced
- 1/2 cup rolled oats
- 1 cup almond milk (or any milk of choice)
- 1/2 tsp ground cinnamon
- 1 tbsp almond butter
- 1 tbsp chia seeds
- A drizzle of honey or maple syrup (optional)

Instructions:

1. **Cook the Oats**: In a pot, bring almond milk to a simmer. Add rolled oats and cook until soft and creamy.
2. **Prepare the Pear**: In a separate pan, sauté diced pear with a sprinkle of cinnamon until softened (about 3-4 minutes).
3. **Assemble the Bowl**: Spoon the cooked oats into a bowl. Top with sautéed pears, almond butter, chia seeds, and a drizzle of honey or syrup.
4. **Serve**: Serve warm for a comforting and flavorful breakfast.

Tropical Fruit Yogurt Bowl

Ingredients:

- 1 cup Greek yogurt (or dairy-free yogurt)
- 1/2 cup pineapple chunks
- 1/2 banana, sliced
- 1/4 cup mango cubes
- 1 tbsp shredded coconut
- Granola for topping

Instructions:

1. **Prepare the Fruit**: Chop the tropical fruits (pineapple, banana, mango) into bite-sized pieces.
2. **Assemble the Bowl**: Spoon the Greek yogurt into a bowl. Arrange the tropical fruits on top.
3. **Top the Bowl**: Sprinkle with shredded coconut and granola for crunch.
4. **Serve**: Serve chilled for a refreshing, tropical breakfast.

Coconut Almond Oats Bowl

Ingredients:

- 1/2 cup rolled oats
- 1 cup coconut milk (or any milk of choice)
- 1 tbsp almond butter
- 2 tbsp shredded coconut
- 1 tbsp sliced almonds
- A drizzle of honey or maple syrup (optional)

Instructions:

1. **Cook the Oats**: In a pot, bring coconut milk to a simmer. Add the oats and cook until soft and creamy.
2. **Add Almond Butter**: Stir in almond butter for extra richness.
3. **Assemble the Bowl**: Spoon the oats into a bowl. Top with shredded coconut, sliced almonds, and a drizzle of honey or maple syrup for sweetness.
4. **Serve**: Serve warm for a cozy, nutty breakfast.

Roasted Banana Oatmeal Bowl

Ingredients:

- 1 banana, sliced
- 1/2 cup rolled oats
- 1 cup almond milk (or any milk of choice)
- 1/2 tsp ground cinnamon
- 1 tbsp peanut butter (optional)
- Chopped walnuts for topping

Instructions:

1. **Roast the Banana**: Preheat the oven to 375°F (190°C). Place banana slices on a baking sheet and roast for 10-12 minutes, until golden and caramelized.
2. **Cook the Oats**: In a pot, bring almond milk to a simmer. Add rolled oats and cook until soft and creamy. Stir in cinnamon.
3. **Assemble the Bowl**: Spoon the oats into a bowl. Top with the roasted banana slices, a dollop of peanut butter (if desired), and chopped walnuts.
4. **Serve**: Serve warm for a comforting and filling breakfast.

Acai and Almond Butter Smoothie Bowl

Ingredients:

- 1 packet frozen acai puree
- 1/2 banana, frozen
- 1/2 cup almond milk (or any milk of choice)
- 1 tbsp almond butter
- 1 tbsp chia seeds
- Granola, sliced fruit, and nuts for topping

Instructions:

1. **Blend the Smoothie**: In a blender, combine frozen acai puree, frozen banana, almond milk, and almond butter. Blend until smooth and thick.
2. **Assemble the Bowl**: Pour the smoothie into a bowl.
3. **Top the Bowl**: Add granola, sliced fruit, nuts, and chia seeds on top.
4. **Serve**: Serve immediately for a creamy and energizing breakfast.

www.ingramcontent.com/pod-product-compliance
Lightning Source LLC
LaVergne TN
LVHW081332060526
838201LV00055B/2592